Waiting in Joyful Hope

*Daily Reflections for
Advent and Christmas
2013–2014*

Jay Cormier

LITURGICAL PRESS

Collegeville, Minnesota

www.litpress.org

Nihil Obstat: Reverend Robert Harren, *Censor deputatus.*
Imprimatur: ✛ Most Reverend John F. Kinney, J.C.D., D.D., Bishop of St. Cloud, Minnesota, May 11, 2012.

Cover design by Ann Blattner. Photo: Thinkstock.

ISSN 1550-803X

ISBN 978-0-8146-3478-3

Introduction

But you, Bethlehem-Ephrathah
   least among the clans of Judah,
From you shall come forth for me
   one who is to be ruler in Israel . . .
He shall take his place as shepherd
   by the strength of the Lord,
   by the majestic name of the Lord, his God;
And they shall dwell securely, for now his greatness
   shall reach to the ends of the earth:
   he shall be peace. (Micah 5:1, 3-4, NABRE)

The Bethlehem of gospel times was a bustling little village at the crossroads of the great caravan routes of the East. Bethlehem was a stopover where business was conducted quickly, camels were changed, horses watered and rested; travelers would stop to eat and spend the night in a small, crowded, uncomfortable inn. Besides the shepherds who grazed sheep on the region's hillsides, the few permanent residents of Bethlehem made their living serving the needs of those passing through. The hometown of King David (Bethlehem's one great claim to fame) had become a busy depot of constant comings and goings.

And yet, as the gospels chronicle, it is in the midst of this busy, hidden little place that God touches human history; in the Christmas moment, God transforms a cave used as a barn, a stable in a small backwater town, into the holiest of shrines, the most sacred of places.

God continues to come down and make his dwelling in unexpected places, transforming our own busy, overwhelmed Bethlehem stables into repositories of his compassion and forgiveness. Like the mobile population of Bethlehem, we are so taken up with the comings and goings in our lives that we fail to realize the presence of God in our midst. But in the weeks ahead, if we stop and look, we can rediscover God in the middle of our frantic homes, our messy lives, our hearts crowded with the constant worries and raw hurts that reside there.

This year's edition of *Waiting in Joyful Hope* includes stories and images of God appearing in the unlikeliest of places, of love being born unexpectedly in our earthy stables and messy barns. We hope these pages help you experience the glad tidings of peace and joy as you ready your own Bethlehem for the coming of the Christ this Christmas. God comes to every "meek soul" who receives him, touching every life with "the wondrous gift" of heaven's peace.

May the words of Phillips Brooks's carol be realized in the Bethlehem of your own home and heart:

Yet in thy dark streets shineth the everlasting Light;
The hopes and fears of all the years are met in thee tonight.

FIRST WEEK OF ADVENT

The Wait

Readings: Isa 2:1-5; Rom 13:11-14; Matt 24:37-44

Scripture:
"[S]tay awake!
For you do not know on which day your Lord will come."
   (Matt 24:42)

Reflection: A young wife and her infant daughter can barely contain themselves as they wait. Any moment now her husband's unit will march into the arena after a year in Afghanistan. They've talked every day via Skype, so at least she knew he had made it through another day; he saw images on his laptop of their little Sarah, who was born after he left—he has yet to hold his daughter.

The waiting began with the first word that his unit would be called up; the waiting took on new urgency as he made arrangements for the family's care during his absence. Waiting was part of the couple's everyday routine until they made their daily Skype connection—and if it was late or delayed, the waiting became unbearable for her. Their waiting became expectation as the day approached when he would come home.

Now, finally arrives the day they have been waiting for what seems like an eternity. Their eyes meet the moment he enters the arena. A few more minutes for the formal dismissal

. . . wait, wait, wait. And the long wait melts when husband and father, wife and mother, and beautiful daughter are in each other's arms again.

They go home, happily awaiting the next chapter of their life together as a family.

Such experiences of waiting are part of all our lives. This season of Advent reminds us that waiting is often the cost of love: In waiting for someone, our own everyday business becomes almost meaningless as we anticipate, worry, and prepare for our loved one's return. In waiting, we realize our own powerlessness; we realize our deepest hopes and needs; we realize the gift the person we are awaiting is to us.

May our waiting for the coming of the Holy One this Christmas help us understand and carry on the mystery of compassionate and generous waiting in our lives.

Meditation: What has been your most difficult experience of waiting? In the end, how was your long vigil rewarded?

Prayer: Come, Lord, and fill our hearts with Advent hope so that we may learn to cope with the delays and disappointments we encounter with patience and wisdom. May a spirit of gratitude and humility guide us on our journey to your dwelling place, enabling us to endure, with joy, the costs of waiting for love, reconciliation, and peace.

December 2: Monday of the First Week of Advent

Keeping Vigil

Readings: Isa 4:2-6; Matt 8:5-11

Scripture:
"Lord, I am not worthy to have you enter under my roof;
only say the word and my servant will be healed."
  (Matt 8:8)

Reflection: It has been a long night. A soft light in the outer
room glows like twilight into the bedroom. Her children sit
quietly in the hall outside, taking turns coming in and holding her hand, carefully wiping her forehead and face, speaking in whispers and barely choking back tears: "Is there
anything I can do for you, Mom? It's OK, Mom. We're here.
We love you."

Her illness has run its course; the doctors can do nothing
more for her. But this night's long vigil actually began many
months before, with the final diagnosis. After the shock and
the tears and the anger came acceptance. She put her financial affairs in order and made clear her wishes regarding
final arrangements.

Once she was ready for death, she started to live. Her
family became the center of her days. With gentleness and
compassion, she healed family rifts, restored friendships,
sought forgiveness for the slights and embarrassments that
mar every life. Though weakened in body, her spirit soared.

Now the final moments of their vigil. By morning, all would be completed. With mumbled prayers on their lips, tears in their eyes, her family cradles her in their love as they commend her to the God who breathed life into her soul seventy-eight years before.

Such an experience is to understand the meaning of this Advent season: These four weeks remind us that every day of our lives is a vigil, a time for putting things in order in preparation for our return to God. God gives us this life—this Advent—so that we might discover him in the love of family and friends and the goodness of this time and world. In the Advent of our lives we make our way to life in and with God in eternity.

Meditation: When have you discovered God during a particularly stressful time of change or unbearable period of waiting?

Prayer: Come, O Christ, Healer and Worker of Wonders! May we trust in your Word to heal our afflictions and illnesses; may we hope in your light to shatter the darkness of our despair and pain. Let us live the Advent of our lives with faith in your compassion, trust in your grace, and hope in your Easter promise.

December 3: Saint Francis Xavier, Priest

The Gift of "Long Walk"

Readings: Isa 11:1-10; Luke 10:21-24

Scripture:
"I give you praise, Father, Lord of heaven and earth,
for although you have hidden these things
from the wise and the learned
you have revealed them to the childlike." (Luke 10:21)

Reflection: One Christmas a boy in an African village gave
his teacher an exquisite seashell as a gift. He had walked
many miles to find it, to a special place along the bay, the
only place such shells could be found.

The teacher was quite moved by the boy's gift: "What a
beautiful shell. You must have walked many miles for it. I
am deeply grateful for your gift," the teacher said.

"Teacher," the boy said, "long walk part of gift."

The young gift-giver possesses the simple but profound
"childlike" faith that Jesus prays his disciples will embrace.
Such faith is centered in the "hidden" values of humility and
compassion. It does not separate words and actions; it
struggles to love as God loves, without limit or condition.
Childlike faith is never discouraged, never becomes cynical
or jaded, never ceases to be amazed and grateful for the
many ways God reveals his presence in our lives. The power
of such simple faith is its ability to overcome every rationali-

zation, fear, and complication in order to mirror the selflessness, integrity, and generosity of Christ Jesus.

   Especially at this busy time of the year, we can be overwhelmed with the shopping, the mailing, the addressing,
the decorating. Remember what the young student under-
stands: that the "long walk" is as much a part of the love we
give and receive as the destination, that the best Christmas
presents are those of the heart and spirit.

Meditation: What gifts have you received that moved you,
not by the object given, but by the time, the planning, the
"long walk" that went into the gift?

Prayer: As we anticipate your coming to us as a humble child
this Christmas, Lord Jesus, help us to embrace your gospel
with simple, childlike faith: faith that is centered in humble
gratitude for the gift of life itself; faith that inspires us to
embrace your Spirit of understanding compassion; faith that
is focused on making your Father's kingdom of reconciling
peace a reality in our time and place.

Perfect Gifts

Readings: Isa 25:6-10a; Matt 15:29-37

Scripture:
Great crowds came to [Jesus],
> having with them the lame, the blind, the deformed, the
> mute,
> and many others.
They placed them at his feet, and he cured them.
> (Matt 15:30)

Reflection: Their teenage daughter had taken up the flute. She had always loved the soft sound of the reed and begged her parents for lessons. Mom and Dad were a little skeptical at first—was this a passion or a passing?—so they found an inexpensive, used instrument for her to get started with.

She quickly developed a real love for the flute and approached each week's lesson with dedication and enthusiasm. Her teacher was excited about her progress—she played beautifully, the teacher said; she was developing a real "feel" for the instrument and had the potential to be a superb player.

So Mom and Dad decided to stretch their Christmas budget to purchase a better flute for their daughter. It was not easy, but this Christmas gift was more than an instrument: it was an affirmation of their daughter's hard work and a sign of their love and support for her dream.

The best Christmas presents are gifts that express the love and support of the giver; the most meaningful presents we give inspire and affirm the best of the receiver. In today's gospel, the evangelist Matthew chronicles the healing works of Jesus. He not only heals broken bodies but also mends broken hearts; he not only restores sight but expands vision as well; he not only feeds the hungry but nourishes their souls too. In the gifts we give and the hospitality we extend this Christmas, may we seek to imitate the compassion of Christ the healer, of Christ who feeds us with the bread of life: may our gift giving be small but effective miracles of God's love in our midst.

Meditation: In what specific ways can the stories of Jesus' healings and the miracle of the loaves and fish inspire your Christmas shopping this year?

Prayer: Lord Jesus, may your compassion be the gift we give this Christmas. Take the pieces of bread and fish that we are able to give and transform them into sacraments of your compassion for those we love. May we work "miracles" of healing and restoration this Christmas; through our acts of generosity and forgiveness, may our families and communities rediscover your loving presence in our midst.

Dance a Little Closer

Readings: Isa 26:1-6; Matt 7:21, 24-27

Scripture:
"Everyone who listens to these words of mine and acts on
     them
   will be like a wise man who built his house on rock."
     (Matt 7:24)

Reflection: *Rose Is Rose* is cartoonist Pat Brady's delight-
ful—and often insightful—chronicle of the Gumbo family:
Rose, her husband Jimbo, and their beloved little son
Pasquale.

In one episode, Mom and Dad are having coffee in the
kitchen late one night when six-year-old Pasquale comes
downstairs. He can't sleep. Something has upset him. The
little boy seems terribly worried. So he asks, "Mom and Dad,
please do a slow dance while the little radio plays softly."

Mom and Dad happily oblige. They turn on the kitchen
radio and find a station playing a slow love song. Dad takes
Mom into his arms, Mom lovingly places her head on Dad's
shoulder, and the couple dances to the soft melody. Little
Pasquale's face lights up with a big smile. "That's perfect,"
he says. Then he yawns and says, "Good night, Mom and
Dad. I love you!" and happily returns to bed.

Mom and Dad say, "Sweet dreams, Pasquale. We love you."

And they continue to dance.

Swaying to the music, Mom says, "He has funny ways of feeling secure."

Dad, still savoring the romance of the moment, replies, "They work for me."

Knowing that we are loved, that we are cared for, is the ultimate security. The parable of the house built on rock resonates during this Christmas season when we are especially aware of our families and loved ones. Our families are meant to be safe places of love and security, our own "Nazareths" where the love of God is reborn every day. God speaks to us in the love, compassion, and forgiveness of our families. Sometimes that love is spoken in near-perfect joy; at other times, that love cries out in desperate pain. Renewed by the joy of Christmas, may we be the reassuring and comforting love of Christ for one another in every season of the year.

Meditation: How are your family and home a place of love and support for one another?

Prayer: O God, be the rock on which we build our lives. Open our hearts and spirits to hear you in the voices of one another. Help us to confront the pain and hurt our selfishness causes those we love and to understand how our failure to love and forgive destroys the houses we have built for our families. By your wisdom and grace, may we realize that we are never alone, that in life's most destructive storms you are with us in the love and forgiveness of family and friends.

Keeping an Eye Out for Turtles

Readings: Isa 29:17-24; Matt 9:27-31

Scripture:
When he entered the house,
   the blind men approached him and Jesus said to them,
   "Do you believe that I can do this?"
"Yes, Lord," they said to him.
Then he touched their eyes and said,
   "Let it be done for you according to your faith."
      (Matt 9:28-29)

Reflection: In her book *The Sacred Meal*, Nora Gallagher tells the story of a new bishop who began his ministry by driving to all the parishes in his vast diocese to meet his priests and communicants. He spent the hours driving from parish to parish listening to all kinds of educational tapes and recorded books, believing it was important to be an informed, educated bishop. And when he arrived at the church he was visiting, "he would basically disgorge onto the people everything he had just learned." From the looks on people's faces, however, he could see it wasn't working.

> One morning, as he was driving [to his next parish], he saw ahead of him a shape on the road. Drawing closer, he saw it was a box turtle. He braked, got out, picked up the turtle, and placed him safely on the other side. As he continued to visit parishes, he started keeping his eye out for turtles, and

there were a lot of them, on or near the roads, in need of rescue. It became his practice to watch for them, and to stop and pick them up if they needed help.

After a while, he stopped listening to the tapes because he might miss a turtle, and he started leaving the windows open so he could smell the air, especially in the early summer. [The bishop] discovered that he was more relaxed and attentive when he arrived at a parish, and this was what people needed and wanted rather than his version of the latest theology.

In "looking out" for turtles, the bishop rediscovered the compassion and consolation that is the heart of his ministry to the people of his diocese. In the busyness of our lives (especially during these hectic days before Christmas), we can become blind to the people who mean the most to us and to the pursuits that bring joy and meaning to our lives; in the many demands placed on us, we stop seeing the possibilities for doing good and affirming things.

Christ comes to restore our "sight," enabling us to realize the presence of God in our lives and to recognize the opportunities God gives us to restore and heal by the grace of that presence.

Meditation: How can faith change the way you "see" Christmas this year?

Prayer: O healing Christ, come into our hearts and homes this Advent. Open our eyes to the light of your compassion; restore our tired spirits so that we may hope again in the possibilities for resurrection in the brokenness of our lives.

December 7:
Saint Ambrose, Bishop and Doctor of the Church

One More Christmas Present

Readings: Isa 30:19-21, 23-26; Matt 9:35–10:1, 5a, 6-8

Scripture:
Jesus sent out these twelve after instructing them thus,
  "Go to the lost sheep of the house of Israel.
As you go, make this proclamation: 'The Kingdom of
  heaven is at hand.' " (Matt 10:6-7)

Reflection: Could you buy an extra gift for someone this Christmas? There are many charities and social service agencies that welcome toys, books, and clothing to help make Christmas a little brighter and merrier for those in need.

So add an extra gift to your shopping list. Select a gift thoughtfully, deliberately (check with the charities and agencies first—they usually have suggestions and are aware of specific needs you can provide for). But, as you shop, try to *see* the person who will be receiving your gift: imagine the struggles, the fears, the constant hopelessness that are part of his or her everyday existence. Put as much time and thought into that gift as you put into a gift for your spouse or child or loved one.

Then do one more thing. Take the receipt for the gift, put it in an envelope, and place the envelope on a branch of your Christmas tree, or near the family manger scene, or on your family table. Make that person who will receive your gift—whom you will never meet or know—a part of your Christmas celebration. Include him or her in the prayers you offer in joy for the coming of the Christ. In your generosity and prayer, you can make God's kingdom a reality for your Christmas "guest."

Meditation: Who might receive your "extra" Christmas present? How could you make that gift a family experience or project?

Prayer: O healing Lord, help us to realize this Advent our own "authority" to bring healing and hope to others. By our simple and unremarkable efforts to live your gospel of humble generosity, may we "drive out" the demons of despair, raise up the fallen and stumbling, and restore the lost and abandoned to hope in the coming of your kingdom.

SECOND WEEK OF ADVENT

December 8: Second Sunday of Advent

Midday Reality Check

Readings: Isa 11:1-10; Rom 15:4-9; Matt 3:1-12

Scripture:
It was of [John] that the prophet Isaiah had spoken when
  he said:
  A voice of one crying out in the desert,
  Prepare the way of the LORD,
    make straight his paths. (Matt 3:3)

Reflection: Kathleen Norris recounts the following scene in
her book *Acedia & Me: A Marriage, Monks, and a Writer's Life*:
  It is the noon rush at a busy downtown restaurant. A man
sipping a drink and chatting with associates begins to cough;
suddenly, he stops breathing and turns blue before collaps-
ing. "In that instant, everything changes. Strangers drop
what they are doing." Someone phones 911, while a group
of waiters, patrons, and friends work together to place the
man on his side to help him breathe again. "When he opens
his eyes and responds, however feebly, to a question, everyone cheers. It is as if time had been suspended, waiting for
this moment. When the EMTs arrive, the rescuers drift back
to their lunches. Having been shocked by the real—forcibly
reminded that life is both precious and precarious, a tenuous
matter of heartbeat and breath—one [patron] will order a
stiff drink, another will phone her husband to tell him that

she loves him. A man will go back to his office and stare at the family photographs on his desk until tears well up. Eventually he will turn to the blinking cursor on his computer screen."

The effect of John the Baptizer's preaching of a baptism of repentance and conversion of life mirrors what happened in that restaurant: the sobering realization that our time is limited, that life is precious and fragile, that the busyness of our days distracts us from the true joys of our lifetimes. John calls us to snap out of our obliviousness to God in our midst. The same Word that came to John in the desert comes to each of us in the deserts of our own hearts, enabling us to transform the wastelands and straighten the winding roads of our lives in the compassion and justice of God.

Meditation: When was the last time you were aware that your life is precious and limited?

Prayer: Come, O Lord, into the Advent of our lives. May your presence in our hearts and homes make us realize the preciousness of the time you have given us. Help us to embrace John's call to be about the work of our baptisms: to create your kingdom of justice, reconciliation, and peace in our time and place.

God Interrupts

Readings: Gen 3:9-15, 20; Eph 1:3-6, 11-12; Luke 1:26-38

Scripture:
"Behold, I am the handmaid of the Lord.
May it be done to me according to your word." (Luke 1:38)

Reflection: In an essay for *The Christian Century*, Lauren Winner reflects on Mary's response to the call to be the Mother of God, a call that was first made manifest in Mary's own immaculate conception.

> I have often wondered what I would have said in Mary's shoes. Would I have said "Fiat mihi"? I doubt it. . . . The fact is, I'm not especially interested in being interrupted by God. God's plans seem rarely to coincide with my own . . .
>
> Actually, I'm better at grand, earthquake interruptions—dramatic interruptions that require moving, changing jobs, radically redirecting life plans—than I am at smaller, more quotidian interruptions. It's the smaller interruptions—say, the knock of an unannounced visitor on my office door—that really irk me. When I hear that unexpected knock, I turn my face into a smile and try not to communicate to my visitors that I was in the middle of a really crucial sentence and would they please leave and close the door behind them?

But Professor Winner has discovered that those many interruptions may well be God knocking:

> [Such interruptions] lead to uncomfortable glimmers of self-awareness; they show me to be a prideful control freak who dares to think that whatever I've got on tap for the day is supremely important and who dares to think that I own my own precious time. . . . And it is that hard-to-swallow fruit of humility that allows me to sometimes recognize these interruptions as God's way of gradually schooling me in the grand imperatives of letting go of all I cling to and following Christ.

Our lives are a series of "interruptions" by God—"annunciations," if you will—in which God focuses our attention on his love and mercy, his compassion and grace, in the midst of our busy lives. May God "interrupt" our Christmas with the true joy of the season—and, like Mary, may we say *Fiat mihi* to the interruption; like Mary, may we accept, with gratitude and joy, God's invitation to bring his beloved Son into our Bethlehems and Nazareths.

Meditation: When has an "interruption" in your plans turned out to be a moment of grace, an "annunciation" of God's love in your midst?

Prayer: Gracious God, may we possess the faith and trust of your daughter Mary to say yes to your "interruptions" in our lives, when you call us to make your presence real in our own time and place. In our welcoming of your Son into our homes and hearts, may we embrace the Advent meaning of this gift of time you have given us.

December 10: Tuesday of the Second Week of Advent

The God of Mending

Readings: Isa 40:1-11; Matt 18:12-14

Scripture:
"If a man has a hundred sheep and one of them goes
   astray,
  will he not leave the ninety-nine in the hills
  and go in search of the stray?" (Matt 18:12)

Reflection: Among the insightful tales of the Desert Fathers
of early Christianity is the story of a soldier who approached
a holy monk.

"Does God really accept our acts of repentance?" the soldier,
torn with doubt and guilt, asked.

The monk asked in reply, "Tell me, if your cloak is torn,
do you throw it away?"

"No, of course not," the soldier said. "I mend it and use it
again."

The old monk said, "Well, if you give such care to repair
your torn cloak, will not God seek to mend the torn relationship with his own son or daughter?"

In the gospels, Jesus reveals to us a God of beginnings, a
God who is never satisfied with rejections and terminations
and endings, a God who always seeks and offers fresh starts,
second chances, and clean slates. The coming of God as an
infant at Christmas manifests God's determination to be
reconciled with all his sons and daughters.

Jesus calls each one of us to the vocation of being "good shepherds," of imitating his image of loving servanthood: to bring back the lost, the scattered, and the forgotten; to enable people to move beyond their fears and doubts to become fully human; to willingly pay the price for justice and mercy so that everyone may be welcomed members of the human family.

Seeking out the lost often demands an extraordinary amount of patience and tolerance and the putting aside of our own pain and sense of betrayal. We all have "lost" sheep in our lives who demand more love, monopolize more of our time, take more of our energy than they are reasonably entitled to. They anger us, exhaust us, and sometimes even humiliate us.

But Jesus calls us to the work of "mending"—to take on the hard work of reconciliation and forgiveness that God begins again in the stable at Bethlehem.

Meditation: Is there a "torn" relationship in your life that you would like to mend this Christmas? How might you begin to go about it?

Prayer: Make us prophets of your compassion, heralds of your peace, and shepherds of your providence, O God. Give us the patience and humility to "mend" relationships torn and friendships broken. Help us to create a straight and sure road this Advent by which all of us—the lost, the forgotten, the exiled—may find our way back to you.

December 11: Wednesday of the Second Week of Advent

The Generous Tiger

Readings: Isa 40:25-31; Matt 11:28-30

Scripture:
"Take my yoke upon you and learn from me,
    for I am meek and humble of heart . . .
For my yoke is easy, and my burden light." (Matt 11:29, 30)

Reflection: There is an Arabian fable about a traveler who came upon a fox that had lost its legs. The traveler wondered how the poor creature managed to survive. Then he saw a tiger approach, with meat in its mouth. After eating its fill of the meat, the tiger left the rest for the maimed fox.

The next day, the traveler watched as the tiger returned with food for itself and the fox. The traveler marveled at the generosity of God to provide for a lowly animal. The man thought, *Surely God cares for me, a human being, as much as he cares for a simple animal. I will rest here from my travels and trust in God to provide.*

So the man made himself comfortable under the shade of a great tree and waited. But days passed. God did not appear; neither food nor water were provided. Soon the starving man was at death's door when he heard an angel's voice call to him: "You poor fool! Open your eyes! Do not imitate the disabled fox—become, instead, the generous tiger!"

Jesus calls us to take on the "yoke" and "burden" of the tiger: to imitate Christ's example of selfless service and compassion to the hungry, the needy, the exhausted in our own forests; to be "eagle's wings" for the weary and despairing, the lost and struggling we meet on our own journey. The "yoke" of the gospel is "easy" in the joy it brings to the generous heart; it is made "light" by the love of God that such selfless compassion brings to our own lives and the lives we are able to touch.

Meditation: What can you give to someone this Christmas that can bring joy to you, the giver?

Prayer: Christ Jesus, help us to learn from you humility of heart and generosity of spirit. By your grace, may we imitate your selflessness in the compassion and love that we are able to extend to the poor, the lost, and the struggling in our own Advents.

December 12: Our Lady of Guadalupe (Catholic Church)
Thursday of the Second Week of Advent (Episcopal Church)

God in Unexpected Places

Readings: Zech 2:14-17 or Rev 11:19a; 12:1-6a, 10ab; Luke 1:26-38 or Luke 1:39-47

Scripture:
"The Holy Spirit will come upon you,
  and the power of the Most High will overshadow you.
Therefore the child to be born
  will be called holy, the Son of God." (Luke 1:35)

Reflection: God appears in unexpected places.

God first reveals himself not in the great civilizations of the young world but to a desert sheik named Abram who discerns a singular, holy presence uniting all life.

He is born not in the magnificence of Jerusalem but in the poverty of Bethlehem.

And today we celebrate God's presence in the appearance of Mary, not in the new world cities of gold but in a poor Mexican village. Mary comes not in the image of the beautiful white Madonna but as a *mestiza* of dark complexion and Indian features.

At Christmas, we experience God incarnate: God becomes human in all humanity's struggles, challenges, and anguish. God comes to live and walk with the poor, the powerless, and the victimized. God enters our human condition: he takes on our flesh; he lives our life. In doing so, he raises up the sacred dignity of every human being; he makes every human life sacred and holy.

In the Advent of our everyday lives, God continues to appear in unexpected places: at our dinner tables and at our children's bedtimes, in our grieving and struggles to find our way, in our brightest mornings and darkest nights. God comes again to make his dwelling in our Bethlehems and Tepeyacs; he illuminates our mangers and hovels with his peace and compassion; he transforms our poverty and hopelessness into the promise of his kingdom.

This Christmas, with the insight of Abraham, the wonder of the shepherds, the determination of the magi, and the hope of Juan Diego, may we realize the compassion and peace of God in our midst.

Meditation: In what "unexpected" moments and places of your life have you experienced the presence of God?

Prayer: Come, Lord, and make your dwelling in our midst; come and sanctify the "unexpected," turbulent, complicated Advents we live every day. As your Child was born in the poverty of Bethlehem, may we transform our own mangers into places where his compassion and forgiveness are born every day. As Mary appeared to Juan Diego as a sister to his people, may we recognize you in our midst in the faces of all our brothers and sisters.

December 13: Saint Lucy, Virgin and Martyr

The Challenges of Discipleship

Readings: Isa 48:17-19; Matt 11:16-19

Scripture:
"To what shall I compare this generation?" (Matt 11:16)

Reflection: We can always find reasons not to act. We can rationalize our behavior at the moment. We can develop a sound, reasonable justification to reject whatever is too demanding of us, to avoid what makes us uncomfortable or threatens our comfort zone.

John the Baptizer? *Too austere, a downer, a real buzz-kill. Life shouldn't be so unhappy.*

Jesus? *He's too quick to forgive the sinners he hangs out with. He lets too many things slide. It's all just too touchy-feely. Life is much more complex than Jesus' nice words. Forgiveness is one thing, but what about personal responsibility?*

But Jesus challenges us to look deeper than the surface, to embrace a wisdom much more complete and timeless than the latest and newest, than the conventional wisdom. The gospel of Jesus and the Advent call of John call us to a life of meaning and purpose, of completeness and holiness that, yes, is demanding and disconcerting and uncomfortable.

In today's short parable, Jesus asks us to embrace an "adult" faith, faith that is centered in the realization that we are not the center of the universe, that there exists outside of ourselves a sacred entity that breathes life into our beings and animates all creation. To become an "adult" man and woman of faith begins with gratitude for the gift of life that is of and from God. The love of God starts with the realization of the needs of another, putting our own wants second for the sake of someone else. Christ calls us to a child*like* faith of simplicity and humility, not a child*ish* faith of "even-Stevens" and "me-firsts."

So let us replace our cynicism with a sense of hope; let us see things not through eyes cloudy with disappointment but in the prism of Christ's light; let us embrace the possibilities for restoration and renewal despite the sacrifice and change demanded of us.

Meditation: What do you find is the most difficult and unsettling aspect of faith? What is, for you, the most challenging demand of Jesus' gospel?

Prayer: May your Spirit of truth and wisdom guide us, O Lord, as we negotiate our Advent roads. Help us to see your justice at the root of humankind's most complex questions, your reconciliation as the heart of all relationships, your compassion at work in the most hidden and forgotten places.

December 14:
Saint John of the Cross, Priest and Doctor of the Church

A Vision of Heaven and Hell

Readings: Sir 48:1-4, 9-11; Matt 17:9a, 10-13

Scripture:
"Elijah will indeed come and restore all things;
  but I tell you that Elijah has already come. . . . "
    (Matt 17:11-12)

Reflection: A great warrior once went to seek the counsel of a humble monk.

"Father," he said, in a voice accustomed to immediate obedience, "teach me about heaven and hell!"

The monk looked up at this mighty commander and replied with utter disdain, "Teach you about heaven and hell? I couldn't teach you about anything! You know nothing—you're all physical might but possess no intellect at all. You're just an arrogant, dirty, wicked thug. Go away—there's nothing I can teach a man like you."

The warrior was stunned. He had never been spoken to like that by anyone. Speechless with humiliation and shaking with rage, the warrior drew his sword and raised it above his head, ready to slay the monk.

"That's hell," the monk explained softly.

The warrior was overwhelmed by the compassion and humility of the little monk who had risked his life to show him hell. He slowly put down his sword, overcome with gratitude for the monk's response. The commander was suddenly at peace.

"And that's heaven," the monk said.

We can create hell right here and now in our judging and condemning those who do not meet our standard of what is right and good, in letting pride and vengeance prevent us from forgiving and seeking forgiveness. And we can experience heaven in imitating the compassion, love, and dedication to reconciliation of the gospel of Jesus. As disciples of Jesus, we are called to be reconcilers, not judges; we are called to forgive, not keep score; we are called to welcome back those who want to return and to enable them to put their lives back together, without our setting up conditions or establishing litmus tests to determine their worthiness and sincerity.

The justice of God proclaimed by the great prophet Elijah is restored in our own commitment to what is right and just; the forgiveness preached by John at the Jordan resonates in our own work at reconciliation with God and with one another; the kingdom of God is in our midst in the peace and compassion within our own hearts and homes.

Meditation: How can you reveal "heaven" in your own home and community this Christmas?

Prayer: Make us your prophets in our own time and place, O saving God. Ignite in us the fire of Elijah, that we may proclaim, in our own commitment to ethics and morality, your reign of justice and reconciliation. Open our lips to speak the good news of John, that in our own compassion and humility, we may proclaim your love in our midst.

THIRD WEEK OF ADVENT

December 15: Third Sunday of Advent

Walking among the Reeds

Readings: Isa 35:1-6a, 10; James 5:7-10; Matt 11:2-11

Scripture:
"What did you go out to the desert to see?" (Matt 11:8)

Reflection: You're working sixty to seventy hours a week; you're lucky if you get six hours of sleep a night. Making income cover expenses is becoming a bigger challenge every month and, in the meantime, your spouse and children—the people you live for—are becoming strangers. *What did you go out to the desert to see?*

You juggle a wide network of acquaintances. The e-mails never stop; there's not an empty line in your calendar book; your cell phone is permanently clipped to your ear. But you can't seem to shake the loneliness you feel even when you are standing in a room full of people. While you maintain contact with a host of business associates and colleagues, precious few of them do you consider friends and no one close to being special. *What did you go out to the desert to see?*

Every semester you scan the course offerings: "I need these credits to graduate . . . this class meets at a good time . . . this professor is a nightmare . . . this lecturer is an easy A . . . God, look at this reading list—no way!" *What did you go out to the desert to see?*

Jesus' question takes on particular urgency in the Advent of our lives: As we struggle to make ends meet, have the means become an end in themselves? Have the love and support of family and friends become just another asset? Are we satisfied merely with credentials that we can list on our resumes or do we want to learn, discover new things, expand our understanding? John's call to transform our lives in the things of God and Jesus' gospel of humble compassion certainly resonate in our broken hearts and despairing spirits— but are we willing to take on the hard work of conversion and re-creation?

May we rediscover, in this season of Advent, what we want our lives to become and continue that re-creation in every season of our lives.

Meditation: What one work or relationship in your life has lost its original meaning or purpose? How can you restore it to what it was meant to be?

Prayer: O God, help us to take on the Advent work of restoring our lives to the meaning and joy for which you created them. In your Son's spirit of selfless servanthood, may we refocus our lives on the compassion, forgiveness, and justice on which your kingdom is built.

December 16: Monday of the Third Week of Advent

Gabby

Readings: Num 24:2-7, 15-17a; Matt 21:23-27

Scripture:
[T]he chief priests and the elders of the people approached
    [Jesus]
  as he was teaching and said,
  "By what authority are you doing these things?
And who gave you this authority?" (Matt 21:23)

Reflection: In their book *Gabby: A Story of Courage and Hope*,
Gabrielle Giffords and her husband, astronaut Mark Kelly,
tell the inspiring story of the congresswoman's recovery from
the traumatic brain injury she suffered in January 2011 when
she was shot while meeting with constituents.

Mark Kelly writes that he has been struck at how "our
spouses are often our teachers, guiding us in ways that may
be clear only in retrospect" and recalls a particular moment
when the couple met the renowned British astrophysicist
Stephen Hawking:

> [Dr. Hawking] is paralyzed due to a form of Lou Gehrig's
> disease. It takes him an excruciatingly long time to say any-
> thing, and I pretty much gave up on conversing with him
> beyond a few pleasantries. But Gabby was just incredible.
> She intuitively knew what to do.

After my failed attempt at interacting with Dr. Hawking, she kneeled down in front of his wheelchair and said, "Dr. Hawking, how are you today?" She then stared into his eyes and waited. As far as she was concerned there was no one else in the crowded room. She waited silently and patiently. Using a device that tracks the motion of a single facial muscle, he took at least ten minutes to compose and utter the phrase "I'm fine. How are you?" Gabby was in no rush. She could have kneeled there for an hour, waiting for his answer. I was so impressed.

After Gabby was injured, I found myself thinking about her encounter with Dr. Hawking. In fact, that memory helped me understand how I'd need to interact with her. . . . It was as if Gabby was giving me a message back in 2006: "Watch me. I will be your teacher. Someday, you'll have to be patient with me and this is how you'll need to do it."

Mark learned patience from Gabby in the same way that Jesus' hearers learn from Jesus' example of compassion and justice. In the "authority" of her own patience and understanding for others, Gabby "teaches" her husband to do the same. Jesus, in the "authority" of his example of humble service, teaches and inspires us to embrace his call to follow him.

Meditation: Who, in your life, have you come to respect as an "authority" in living your faith?

Prayer: Rabbi Jesus, teach us the things of God. Let your word of justice and peace take root in our spirits; light the lamp of your wisdom in our hearts so that we may see our world and one another in the clear light of your love.

"Deck the Halls"

Readings: Gen 49:2, 8-10; Matt 1:1-17

Scripture:
The book of the genealogy of Jesus Christ,
   the son of David, the son of Abraham. (Matt 1:1)

Reflection: If you haven't already, in the next day or two you will be hauling out the boxes of Christmas decorations.

In some homes, Christmas trees are living family records, adorned with small photos, with ornaments marking births and graduations and marriages, with decorations made by family members over the years. At the end of the holidays, the ornaments are packed away with great care in order to be handed on from parent to child to grandchild to great-grandchild.

Simple things like Christmas decorations remind us of our connectedness to one another and to those who came before us. Photos, letters, yearbooks, and mementos remind us of our roots, how our identities and values are the result of the wisdom and love of those who came before us.

Every moment of our lives is connected in time—one memory is the entry to another, one event sets the stage for the next. Today's gospel is a connection of such memories: the evangelist Matthew reminds us that the story of Jesus begins with the uncompromising, powerful love of God—

love that was the creative force of the first Genesis and is now the perfection of the second Genesis. And so, Matthew begins his gospel with an account of Jesus' ancestry.

While the accuracy of his list is dubious, Matthew's chronicle underscores the evangelist's point that this Jesus is the fulfillment of a world that God envisioned from the first moment of creation—a world created in the justice and peace that is the very nature and substance of its Creator. It is a vision that includes desert nomads and kings, shepherds and farmers, craftsmen and peasants, saints and sinners. It is a vision that transcends geography and culture and status—and even time itself.

And it is a vision that includes all of us—and our children and grandchildren and their children and grandchildren. As God called Abraham and Judah and Tamar and David and Hezekiah and Eliakim and Joseph and Mary of the first Advent to prepare for the appearance of Christ, God calls us in our own time, in these days of the second Advent, to prepare for the reappearance of Christ in the fulfillment of time.

Meditation: What Christmas decorations and traditions in your family do you especially cherish?

Prayer: God of all times and seasons, you called generations before us to make ready for the dawning of your Christ. Grateful for the faith we have received from them, help us to pass that faith on to our children and our children's children. May the light of your Christ shine on us and our world; by his light, may we and every generation continue the work of restoring your reign of justice and peace.

A Parent's Dreams

Readings: Jer 23:5-8; Matt 1:18-25

Scripture:
"Joseph, son of David,
do not be afraid to take Mary your wife into your home.
For it is through the Holy Spirit
that this child has been conceived in her." (Matt 1:20)

Reflection: From the moment a couple learns they will be parents, they begin to dream about and dream for their child.

The first dreams are for a safe birth, a strong and complete body, good health and physical development. Then parents dream that their son or daughter will excel in sports, master the sciences, distinguish themselves in the arts and literature. They may even dare to dream that their child will one day be elected president, quarterback the 49ers, sing at the Met, or conquer Wall Street.

Along the way, of course, the dreams will change. Where they once dreamt about the Nobel Prize, Mom and Dad will now settle for passing algebra. The dream of a World Series ring is quickly forgotten when anguished parents wait and hope that their son will walk again or that their daughter will wake up after a horrible accident. The dream of a Bill Gates-like fortune is set aside when terrified parents desperately wait for their child's safe return from a dangerous sojourn into the world of drugs, sex, and violence.

Fear, disappointment, adversity, and tragedy change our more grandiose dreams for our children. But, as Joseph learns from his dreams, the most important things we can dream for our children are wisdom, happiness, and peace—all gifts our children can first experience within the safety and support of loving families.

In this Christmas season and in every season, may Joseph be our model for making those dreams a reality: like Joseph, may we possess the openness of heart and spirit to behold God's presence in all things; like Joseph, may we possess the humility and selflessness to seek understanding and acceptance within our families even at the cost of our own expectations and hopes; like Joseph, may we possess the courage and commitment to be sources of affirmation and support for our spouses and children.

Meditation: What "dream" do you most wish to see fulfilled for your family? What can you do to realize that dream?

Prayer: May your Spirit, O God, come down upon us with the wisdom to understand your "dream" for us and the grace to realize that dream: to become your people of compassion and generosity, brothers and sisters bound together in your love, your church of reconciliation and forgiveness.

December 19: Thursday in Late Advent

"Who, Me?"

Readings: Judg 13:2-7, 24-25a; Luke 1:5-25

Scripture:
Zechariah said to the angel,
  "How shall I know this?
For I am an old man, and my wife is advanced in years."
  (Luke 1:18)

Reflection: We all have our Zechariah moments when things just seem impossible, out of sync with our expectations, unreasonable and absurd.

How can God expect me—me?!—to be able to do this? Me—incompetent, talentless, sinful little me?!

The story of Zechariah is about those fears and the inability to trust in God and in ourselves that we all experience. Zechariah—ironically, a priest of the temple and, presumably, a man of great faith—cannot believe Gabriel's news that he and his beloved Elizabeth will be the parents of a child. Faced with such an overwhelming prospect, he is terrified because of his age and that of his wife; he is unable to trust in the God he has so faithfully taught and served. So the angelic messenger takes away Zechariah's ability to speak—Zechariah will regain his speech only when all that God has promised will come to pass.

But God calls every one of us—Zechariahs all—to bring his justice and mercy to birth in our own time and place.

Sometimes we need a Gabriel to remind us not to worry or be afraid, to put aside our doubts and fears and allow ourselves to hope, to realize the possibilities we have for doing good, for acting justly, for being the means for reconciliation and healing. God gives us his grace to speak his word of compassion and peace if we trust in that compassion and peace, if we are willing to pay the price for those words as God has paid the price for those words, if we remain faithful to the God who remains faithful to us.

As Zechariah learns, sometimes it's a matter of being quiet and doing the hard work of hope.

Meditation: When have you hesitated to take on some act of generosity or take the initiative in restoring a relationship because you felt it was beyond your ability?

Prayer: Help us, O Lord, to put aside the fears and doubts that prevent us from bringing your compassion and peace to birth in our own homes. Still our spirits, quiet our hearts, so that we may always find reason to hope and believe that reconciliation and love are always possible, despite our doubts and cynicism.

Bringing God to Birth

Readings: Isa 7:10-14; Luke 1:26-38

Scripture:
Mary said, "Behold, I am the handmaid of the Lord.
May it be done to me according to your word." (Luke 1:38)

Reflection: A seven-year-old works quietly and patiently at her desk making her own Christmas card for her mom.

A mother is up late one night preparing a "care package" of homemade cookies and bread to get her son, a college freshman, through his first set of final exams.

A grandmother works early in the morning, when her arthritic fingers are at their nimblest, to knit scarves for her grandchildren.

Dad spends hours searching through travel websites to find a deal on a trip to Disney World in the spring to surprise his family.

Teenagers spend several evenings getting the parish hall ready to host a weekend Christmas party for children from struggling families assisted by the local Catholic social services agency.

In the precious time they give, in their focus to bring the joy of Christmas to someone, all of these good folks echo Mary's yes to God's call to "give birth" to his Christ, to bring forth the peace of the Savior, to enable the Spirit of God to do its work of embracing everyone in the love of God. Gabriel may come in the form of an invitation, a plea, a concern for another's well-being; Mary's yes may take the form of time given, generosity extended, forgiveness offered. In the Advents of our lives, God calls us to bring his Christ into our own time and place; may we respond with the faith and trust of Mary, putting aside our own doubts and fears to say, "I am your servant, O God. Be it done as you say."

Meditation: What can you do this Christmas that can be your yes to God's call to you to "give birth" to his Christ?

Prayer: O Lord, our Father and Redeemer, may we realize the many ways you "announce" to us your presence in our lives and your invitation to "give birth" to your compassion and peace in our midst. May your Spirit instill in us the generosity of heart and perseverance of spirit to let your call to your work of compassion and reconciliation "be done" in our homes and hearts.

December 21: Saturday in Late Advent

Las Posadas

Readings: Song 2:8-14 or Zeph 3:14-18a; Luke 1:39-45

Scripture:
Elizabeth, filled with the Holy Spirit,
cried out in a loud voice and said,
"Most blessed are you among women,
and blessed is the fruit of your womb." (Luke 1:41-42)

Reflection: On these last evenings before Christmas, our Latino brothers and sisters celebrate *Las Posadas*, the feast of "the inns."

In many Latino communities, on the nine evenings before Christmas, the "holy pilgrims" Mary and Joseph travel each night from house to house, seeking a place to stay on their journey to Bethlehem. In some communities, a couple plays the part of the pilgrims, with Mary riding a little donkey led by Joseph; in others, statues of Mary and Joseph are carried through the streets. Those accompanying the holy pilgrims carry lanterns in procession, singing songs and offering prayers as Mary and Joseph look for shelter.

When they come to a house, the family residing there proudly makes reparation for the old refusal. "Come into our humble home, and welcome!" the host family proclaims, "and may the Lord give shelter to my soul when I leave this world." The family opens their doors and welcomes all who accompany Mary and Joseph to the feast the household has prepared. Different homes and families are visited each evening until Christmas Eve, when *Las Posadas* ends with the celebration of Midnight Mass.

Las Posadas, which began in Mexico in the late sixteenth century, is a time to open the doors of our hearts to give shelter to the Christ who travels among us in the guise of our families and friends, of the poor and needy, of the forgotten and marginalized. In every day and every season of the year, Mary and Joseph and the Holy Child knock on our door looking for shelter, looking for a place to make their home. May our Advent prayer be that we have the wisdom and love to welcome them.

Meditation: How can you make your home a more welcoming place for those who come to your door?

Prayer: God of all times and ages, come and make your dwelling place in our midst. May your love be our house of safety and consolation; may your peace be the table where we gather; may your forgiveness be the hearth that warms us and brings us together.

FOURTH WEEK OF ADVENT

Joseph's House

Readings: Isa 7:10-14; Rom 1:1-7; Matt 1:18-24

Scripture:
"Joseph, son of David,
do not be afraid to take Mary your wife into your home.
For it is through the Holy Spirit
that this child has been conceived in her." (Matt 1:20)

Reflection: The last week of Advent shifts our focus from the promise of the Messiah to the fulfillment of that promise in the events surrounding Jesus' birth.

The gospel for the Fourth Sunday of Advent this year is Matthew's version of Jesus' birth at Bethlehem. This is not Luke's beloved story of a child born in a Bethlehem stable welcomed by humble shepherds and a choir of angels. Matthew's story is much darker. In Matthew's account, Jesus' coming is a disgrace and a scandal; his birth is a source of humiliation, an embarrassment for his family.

The carpenter Joseph is the central figure in Matthew's story. In Matthew's account, Joseph learns that his fiancée is pregnant. Confused and hurt, Joseph, an observant but compassionate Jew, does not wish to subject Mary to the full fury of Jewish law, so he plans to divorce her "quietly." But an angel appears to Joseph in a dream and reveals that this Child is his people's long-awaited Messiah. Because of his complete faith and trust in God's promise, Joseph acknowledges the Child and names him Jesus ("Savior," "deliverer") and becomes, in the eyes of the law, the "legal" father of Jesus.

In Matthew's gospel, Christ's entry into human history begins with the compassion of Joseph the carpenter. Joseph puts aside his own hurt and embarrassment and welcomes the Child as his own. God's birth in our midst depends on human partners like Mary and Joseph who are willing to believe the impossible, to claim the unwanted, to love the helpless and neediest, to dare to hope in Emmanuel—"God is with us."

Every one of us is called to be Joseph—to welcome God in our midst. In the mystery of Christmas, God's *yes* depends on our *yes*.

Meditation: How can you take on the role of Joseph this Christmas by bringing the compassion and forgiveness of God into a difficult and strained situation?

Prayer: O God, help us to build our family's home on the compassion, faith, and trust of Joseph. In times of crisis and tension, bless our families with the hope of your consolation and forgiveness; in times of joy and growth, bless us with a spirit of gratitude, never forgetting that you are the Father of us all, the Giver of all that is good.

December 23: Monday in Late Advent

Making Memories

Readings: Mal 3:1-4, 23-24; Luke 1:57-66

Scripture:
[Zechariah] asked for a tablet and wrote, "John is his
    name,"
    and all were amazed.
Immediately his mouth was opened, his tongue freed,
    and he spoke blessing God. (Luke 1:63-64)

Reflection: In her wonderful book, *My Monastery Is a Mini-van*, Denise Roy shares many entertaining and touching stories of her own family's spiritual journey amid the noise and mess and clutter and chaos that are part of contemporary family life. In one essay, she writes about the most important lesson she has learned as the mother of four:

It is humbling, as a parent, to realize what it is that children remember. All of our many efforts to provide them with fancy gifts or exciting trips may not, in the end, matter as much as the feeling they get when they sit in a tree or on our lap. For all of us, the memories that contain the greatest joys are usually of times when we felt connected—to ourselves, to nature, to our parents, to God. Even though these moments happened many years ago, we continue to carry within us something of their holiness.

It is so easy to not experience such connection. Our busy lives pull us away from ourselves, so much so that we even forget how to breathe. We rarely hold still. Our bodies might be sitting with our children, but our minds are racing off in many other directions. When our little ones look us in the eyes, they know we are not there. . . .

For we teach our children not so much by preaching lessons or dogma to them as by the way we walk and sit and see the world. They will learn to breathe and smile and be compassionate and connected to themselves and to their world through our example.

Children first meet God and encounter the sacred in their parents. All families—Mary, Joseph, and Jesus; Elizabeth, Zechariah, and John; you, your spouse, and your children—are holy places where the love of God dwells. This Christmas, the season of special memories, let us make for our children and families lasting memories of God's love for them; let them see, in our caring, our joy, our forgiveness, the deeper meaning of God becoming human for us.

Meditation: What is your most cherished memory from your own childhood and what does that memory teach you about the things of God?

Prayer: God our Father, come make your dwelling place within our homes this Christmas and every season. May we celebrate your presence in our midst by making for one another memories that reflect your generous love, your healing forgiveness, your lasting peace.

December 24: Tuesday in Late Advent (Christmas Eve)

Zechariah's Song

Readings: 2 Sam 7:1-5, 8b-12, 14a, 16; Luke 1:67-79

Scripture:
"In the tender compassion of our God
  the dawn from on high shall break upon us,
  to shine on those who dwell in darkness and the
    shadow of death,
  and to guide our feet into the way of peace." (Luke 1:79)

Reflection: Today's gospel is one of the most beautiful hymns in all of Scripture.

The elderly Zechariah has struggled to believe Gabriel's news that he and his beloved Elizabeth could be parents in their advanced age—and that their child would become the herald of the long-awaited Messiah. Zechariah is struck mute by God until all that God has promised would happen happens.

And then, Elizabeth gives birth to a little boy. Zechariah realizes what Elizabeth has understood all along: that this child is the work of God. Zechariah professes his trust in God when he announces to the surprise of all that the child is to be named John—the name the angel Gabriel instructed Zechariah to give the child. At that moment, the old priest can speak again and he offers the beautiful canticle that we read in today's Christmas Eve gospel.

Every morning at Lauds in the Liturgy of the Hours, the church prays Zechariah's canticle, giving thanks to God for his wonderful and inexplicable work of salvation and reconciliation.

As you go about your work preparing for tomorrow, let every task express the gratitude of Zechariah and the joy that dawns at Christmas: may you look forward to welcoming your guests to your table in the peace of the Christ Child; may the gifts you wrap and place under your tree today express the love of God in your midst; may the lights and greenery reflect the light and life that dawn in your home and heart.

And let your spirit find reason to sing Zechariah's song every morning of the New Year: may you always realize the many revelations of God's compassion and peace in your life; may your Christmas celebration reverberate throughout 2014 with hope in the possibilities for reconciliation and forgiveness in the simplest and most hidden events of your days.

Meditation: How can you make tomorrow a day of gratitude in the spirit of Zechariah's canticle?

Prayer: In the birth of your Son, O God, you have touched human history. May the dawning of Christ illuminate every morning; may his birth re-create every human heart; may his presence among us transform our own Bethlehems into holy places of your compassion and peace.

SEASON OF CHRISTMAS

December 25: The Nativity of the Lord (Christmas)

Joyeux Noel

Readings:
VIGIL: Isa 62:1-5; Acts 13:16-17, 22-25; Matt 1:1-25
   (or 1:18-25)
MIDNIGHT: Isa 9:1-6; Titus 2:11-14; Luke 2:1-14
DAWN: Isa 62:11-12; Titus 3:4-7; Luke 2:15-20
DAY: Isa 52:7-10; Heb 1:1-6; John 1:1-18 (or 1:1-5, 9-14)

Scripture:
"Glory to God in the highest and on earth peace to those
   on whom his favor rests." (Luke 2:14)

Reflection: It happened on Christmas Eve 1914 during the
First World War.

Three regiments—one French, one Scottish, and one German—had been locked in battle for weeks in the dirty dark
trenches along a French hillside. On Christmas Eve, a truce
was called. As the night began, a German soldier sang "Silent
Night" for his comrades—from the other side of the battle
field, two Scottish bagpipes picked up the accompaniment;
then the pipers began to play "Adeste Fidelis," and the tenor
started to sing along with them. Soon soldiers from each side
peered over "No Man's Land" and cautiously approached
one another. Slowly, tentatively, the troops laid down their
weapons.

The story of this remarkable cease-fire is beautifully told in the 2006 French film *Joyeux Noel*.

The troops exchanged photographs of their wives and girlfriends and shared precious bits of chocolate and champagne. A priest from the Scottish regiment offered Mass in the cold field and all three regiments joined in prayer. On Christmas Day, the two sides happily skirmished in a soccer game. French, Scot, and German soldiers then helped one another bury their dead comrades whose corpses had been rotting between the lines.

But when the war resumed late on Christmas, the three sides could no longer draw weapons against the others. They were no longer enemies—Christmas had transformed them into fellow fathers and sons and farmers and artists and clerks.

The dawning of Christ illuminates our perspective of the world and of one another. In his light, we recognize one another as brothers and sisters and sons and daughters of his heavenly Father. The coming of Christ transforms the hopeless and cynical winter landscape into a new springtime when peace is not only possible but imperative.

Meditation: In what concrete ways can Christmas "peace" transform your perspective and outlook?

Prayer: Welcome, O Child of Bethlehem! Fill our empty hearts with your Father's peace: the peace that heals, that comforts, that lifts up, that unites. And may your Spirit make us ministers of that peace, enabling us to become God's "people of good will"—a people dedicated to building your reign of compassion, justice, and peace for all people, in all seasons.

Boxing Day

Readings: Acts 6:8-10; 7:54-59; Matt 10:17-22

Scripture:
As they were stoning Stephen, he called out
   "Lord Jesus, receive my spirit." (Acts 7:59)

Reflection: In Great Britain, Canada, Australia, and many nations of the British Commonwealth, today is Boxing Day.

Many historians trace the beginning of the holiday to the story told in the Christmas carol "Good King Wenceslaus." Wenceslaus, duke of Bohemia in the early tenth century, was traveling across his vast estates on the day after Christmas, St. Stephen's Day, when he saw a poor man gathering wood in the middle of a snowstorm. The king was so moved by the man's plight that he returned to his castle and gathered up the food and wine left over from the Christmas feast and carried them through the blizzard to the hovel of the poor man.

English churches have a long tradition of collecting alms for the poor during the season of Advent; then, on the day after Christmas, "Boxing" Day, the boxes are opened and the contents distributed to the poor. It was also the custom for great sailing ships to carry a sealed box filled with gold for good luck. If the ship arrived home safely from its voyage, the box would be given to a priest who would open it at

Christmas and use the money inside for the poor of the parish.

Fans of *Upstairs Downstairs* and *Downton Abbey* know that Boxing Day is the traditional day when the British aristocracy distributes gifts (Christmas presents are called "Christmas boxes" in England) to their servants and employees. Because these domestics work on Christmas Day, December 26 is their day to return home and exchange "Christmas boxes" with their families.

The Boxing Day traditions call us to gratitude for God's many blessings during this holy season and in every season of the year. As you continue to enjoy the glow of yesterday's feast, consider all you have to be grateful for on this day after Christmas and prepare your own "Christmas box" for the poor, the forgotten, and the needy, sharing with them the blessings of the Savior's birth.

Meditation: How can you make some part of Boxing Day part of your family's Christmas celebration?

Prayer: Father, we give you thanks for the many blessings we have received. May we express that thanks to you in sharing those blessings with others. Inspired by the gospel of your Son and the example of your saints, Stephen and Wenceslaus, may we readily share our "Christmas boxes" in your spirit of joy, humility, and compassion.

The King's Speech

Readings: 1 John 1:1-4; John 20:1a, 2-8

Scripture:
They both ran, but the other disciple ran faster than Peter
   and arrived at the tomb first;
   he bent down and saw the burial cloths there . . .
[H]e saw and believed. (John 20:4-5, 8a)

Reflection: When David was three years old, he stuttered
badly. Stammering, as it was called in his native England,
was considered a disability, a defect. As David grew older,
his stammering grew more pronounced; the boy became
increasingly isolated.

But it was the age of radio and, for the first time, the English people could actually hear the voice of their sovereign.
David listened to the speeches of King George VI, calling his
countrymen to unite to defend their homeland against the
Nazi war machine. Young David especially was inspired by
the king's speeches—because the king was a stutterer like
David. David realized that being a "stammerer" did not
make him a "defective" person, that the difficulty he had
speaking did not mean that he was stupid. If the king could
find his voice to lead his people, David could find his voice
as well.

And David did.

David Seidler went on to become a successful screenwriter. He resolved someday to write the story of his childhood hero, King George VI. After years of waiting for permission from the royal family, David Seidler wrote the story that has become a source of hope for millions of stutterers around the world—the Academy Award–winning film *The King's Speech.*

David Seidler's *The King's Speech* is a story of newness, of hope, of possibility. It is a story of resurrection, told in the same spirit and with the same resolve that embraces the story of the dawning of the Christ Child at Christmas and the story of Christ's resurrection at Easter. These stories and stories like them also remind us that Christ's resurrection is more than an event: the resurrection is an attitude, a perspective, a light to guide us along this path of stones we stumble along. The resurrection is the love that pulls us out of our tombs of fear and hopelessness; the resurrection is to realize that we are embraced by God in the embrace of one another.

Meditation: In what ways can you tell the "story" of the risen Jesus in your everyday life?

Prayer: O God, in your compassion and peace you have brought resurrection to our Advent lives. May we now become tellers of that story in the compassion we extend and receive, in the gospel principles of justice and forgiveness we struggle to practice, in our own efforts to "make flesh" your Word of reconciliation and peace.

The Deaths of the Innocent

Readings: 1 John 1:5–2:2; Matt 2:13-18

Scripture:
When Herod realized that he had been deceived by the
    magi,
  he became furious.
He ordered the massacre of all the boys in Bethlehem and
    its vicinity
  two years old and under,
  in accordance with the time he had ascertained from the
    magi. (Matt 2:16)

Reflection: Today a firefighter will be killed trying to save someone trapped in a burning building.

Today a police officer will die during a routine traffic stop or a call to break up a fight that goes horribly and unexpectedly wrong.

Today an American serviceman or woman will lose his or her life protecting our peace and that of a people far away.

Today many good and generous souls will give their lives for the sake of others.

They are saints. They are Holy Innocents.

Today we remember the children who were murdered in the wake of Herod's horrific desperation to eliminate the Messiah-King. Every time and place has suffered the loss of innocent men, women, and children who die as a result of injustice, violence, and oppression. Today, we will see and read stories about "innocents" here and now, whose deaths remind us that Herod-like insanity continues to exist, that these times raise up men and women who give their lives for the sake of justice, compassion, and peace.

Today, remember the "Holy Innocents" whose deaths inspire us to embrace the justice and peace of the Messiah, who comes to free us from both the Herods beyond us and the Herods within us.

Meditation: Who are the innocents you know who give their lives for the sake of others, who sacrifice themselves so that others may live?

Prayer: God of mercy, welcome into your presence "the innocents" whose lives are taken from them by the Herods of our own time and place; give places of honor at your heavenly table to "the innocents" who give their lives for their brothers and sisters in you. May their example inspire us to bring comfort and healing, your justice and freedom, to a world broken and enslaved by avarice and ignorance.

Flights to Egypt

Readings: Sir 3:2-6, 12-14; Col 3:12-21 (or 3:12-17); Matt 2:13-15, 19-23

Scripture:
"Rise, take the child and his mother, flee to Egypt,
and stay there until I tell you." (Matt 2:13)

Reflection: It has been a rough year. Dad lost his job a year ago; finding a new one has been a full-time occupation. Mom has taken on a number of part-time jobs while being a full-time mother to their two daughters. The girls have been terrific, helping out in whatever ways they can. Dad was finally offered a position in another city several hundred miles away. They had no choice but to pull up stakes and start over: selling their old house and finding a new one (while Dad had already gone ahead to start with his new company), arranging for schools, packing up, and saying good-bye. That first night together in their new house, surrounded by their life in packing boxes, they sat on the floor and ate Chinese takeout. And they realized not what they had lost but what they had in each other: a home.

It was a long night. Little Jack cried and cried with colic. In shifts, they cradled Jack as they walked up and down the hall, rubbing his little back, singing to him until he finally fell asleep. It was early in the morning when they finally put

Jack down in his crib. They were exhausted but happy that the most precious thing in their lives was peacefully asleep.

It is a difficult conversation. There is no easy way to begin that "talk" with your preteen child, that confrontation with a teenage son or daughter about abusing alcohol or some other substance, that decision regarding an elderly parent's care. The exchange can quickly deteriorate into an angry exchange of recriminations and accusations, resulting in rejection and estrangement. Love often requires us to risk that love for the sake of the beloved.

The financial, physical, and emotional circumstances we face in our lives as spouses and families force us to "flee" to our own Egypts. As is clear from Matthew's gospel, Mary, Joseph, and the Child's struggle as a family was filled with heartache, fear, misunderstanding, and doubt—but together they created a family of love and compassion, of nurture and acceptance.

As we gather as families this Christmas, may we realize anew the demanding but fulfilling work of creating and maintaining that safe place of unconditional love, welcome, and forgiveness that is family.

Meditation: What has been the hardest situation your family has had to deal with? How were you able to cope with it?

Prayer: Loving Father, keep our family within the embrace of your loving providence. In times of crisis and tension, bless our families with the hope of your consolation and forgiveness; in times of joy and growth, bless us with a spirit of thankfulness.

Anna

Readings: 1 John 2:12-17; Luke 2:36-40

Scripture:
There was a prophetess, Anna . . .
She never left the temple,
　but worshiped night and day with fasting and prayer.
And coming forward at that very time,
　she gave thanks to God and spoke about the child
　to all who were awaiting the redemption of Jerusalem.
　　(Luke 2:36, 38)

Reflection: We all know Anna.

She has survived wars and hardships and suffered all manner of intolerance and bigotry. With her late husband, she worked hard and struggled through lean times to raise their family, seeing to it that all her sons and daughters were educated, established, and loved. Now, well into her ninth decade, her greatest joys are the children of her grandchildren. Anna is a source of joy, inspiration, and grace to her family and friends. Every moment of her long, fruitful life has quietly but brilliantly reflected the light of God's love to all.

Anna, whose name means "grace" and "favor," walks among us today within our own "temples." For Luke, the elderly prophetess Anna is an icon of the faithful Jew—the "remnant" (Zeph 3:12) who awaits the coming of the Messiah and the restoration of Israel's covenant of compassion and justice with God. Luke identifies her as a member of the tribe of Asher, a northern clan of Jews who suffered great hardship during the Assyrian occupation of the eighth century BC. She is a familiar figure around the temple who devotes all of her time in prayer and fasting in the women's court of the temple.

Anna possesses the wisdom of God that enables her to realize God's presence in every moment; she also possesses the generosity of heart to make that presence known in the quiet joy and ready compassion she lives. In her graciousness, in her optimism, in her persevering hope, Anna is a prophetess of God's salvation.

There is an Anna in all of our lives—a woman who inspires gratitude and teaches compassion by the lessons of her long life. In the wisdom that comes with age, in the love and care they extend to us in their grace and joy, in their faith made strong and unshakable through a lifetime of struggle, the Annas of our time and place are rays of God's light shining through all of our lives, illuminating the way to God's eternal dwelling place.

Meditation: Who is the "Anna" in your life and what is the most important "prophecy" you have learned from her?

Prayer: O God, open our hearts to receive your Son into our homes and hearts with joyful gratitude. May his presence in our lives enable us to be prophets of your justice and mercy and ministers of your compassion and peace.

December 31: Seventh Day in the Octave of Christmas

An "Incarnate" Teaching Experience

Readings: 1 John 2:18-21; John 1:1-18

Scripture:
And the Word became flesh
and made his dwelling among us, . . . (John 1:14)

Reflection: It was Professor Barbara Brown Taylor's first experience teaching a course via the internet. The college organized a workshop at which she "learned how to post [her] syllabus, establish a chat room, monitor discussions and grade student assignments—all without leaving [her] office." While appreciating the "democratic and ecological advantages" of teaching online, she still could not imagine teaching students whose faces she never saw or whose voices she never heard. She shared her concern with other faculty, but they were all sold on the "cyberspace university." "Some introverted students really blossom online," one said. "You can reach so many people," another assured her.

True, she thought, but there was still something missing for her. Then, it dawned on her:

> "The problem is that I'm a Christian," I said. "I am absolutely sold on the value of incarnation, and there aren't enough pixels in the universe to convince me otherwise." . . . My faith [is] in the redemptive power of flesh-and-blood relationships, which cannot be simulated on any computer screen.

At Christmas, we stand in awe of the God who became one of us. The word "incarnation" means "to become or be made flesh," or "to become enfleshed." In the Christ Child, the sacred is not some abstract concept of theological theory: the love of God has become real to us in this birth. In the incarnation, our God has come to know that our lives are filled with disappointment, pain, and despair; he has lived through the storms and crises we live through; he has given us hope in our world by showing us the way to life in his world.

Christ is the Word of God with a human face, the embodiment of the very love of God—love present in the compassion and forgiveness we extend to one another, love present in our efforts to carry on his work of reconciliation and peace, love present in every act of selflessness that mirrors the "human" face of God.

Meditation: In what everyday experiences are you most aware that God has "been made flesh" and "dwells" in your midst?

Prayer: Christ Jesus, you are the Word that set all creation into motion; you are the Light that illuminates every human life; you are the love of God in flesh and blood. Let your Word echo in our hearts so that we may re-create the world in the Father's compassion; let your light shatter the darkness of sin and alienation; let your love be the glory we seek, as we struggle to imitate your example of humble and grateful service to one another.

Blue Nights

Readings: Num 6:22-27; Gal 4:4-7; Luke 2:16-21

Scripture:
Mary kept all these things,
reflecting on them in her heart. (Luke 2:19)

Reflection: The novelist and essayist Joan Didion's book *Blue Nights* is an elegy to her daughter, Quintana, who died in 2005 after twenty months of failing health. Quintana was thirty-nine.

Ms. Didion writes of her struggle to cope with her daughter's death, while dealing with her own declining health and advancing age. In remembering Quintana, whom she and her husband adopted in 1966, Ms. Didion second-guesses herself as a mother: Did she do her duty by her daughter, did she nurture her, protect her, care for her enough? Did she love her enough? Though her fears are groundless, they are nonetheless very real—as they are for most parents.

In one especially poignant moment, Ms. Didion writes of forcing herself to go through boxes and closets in her New York apartment, filled with once-treasured mementos and souvenirs "I no longer want."

I find more faded and cracked photographs than I want ever again to see.

I find many engraved invitations to the weddings of people who are no longer married.

I find many mass cards from the funerals of people whose faces I no longer remember.

In theory these mementos serve to bring back the moment.

In fact they serve only to make clear how inadequately I appreciated the moment when it was here.

In today's gospel, we hear the story of another mother who is facing her own fears and doubts about parenthood. As both Mary and Joan Didion discover, it is in reflecting on our memories that we realize the presence of God in the many ordinary events and everyday exchanges of our lives. In the midst of our fears and suspicions, in our hurts and misunderstandings, in our feelings of love and loss, in all our days and nights, God is there, transforming our lives in the love revealed in his Christ.

Meditation: What is the hardest, most difficult memory of 2013 that you would like to make better or heal in 2014?

Prayer: O God, Giver of all good things, may we begin this New Year with a spirit of gratitude for the many blessings we have received and a spirit of humility to make the year ahead an opportunity for healing and peace. May our Christmas memories be the beginning of hope for this New Year; may our remembrances of Christmases past teach us your work of compassion and reconciliation.

January 2:
Saints Basil the Great and Gregory Nazianzen, Bishops
and Doctors of the Church

Turtle Crossing

Readings: 1 John 2:22-28; John 1:19-28

Scripture:
John answered them,
 "I baptize with water;
 but there is one among you whom you do not recognize,
 the one who is coming after me,
 whose sandal strap I am not worthy to untie."
 (John 1:27)

Reflection: A road cuts through a large stream near the center of town. The stream is home to birds, fish, and turtles. . . .

On a tree where the road intersects with the stream, there hangs a sign: *TURTLE CROSSING—Be careful.* A second sign is posted warning drivers coming from the opposite direction as well.

The signs were not posted by the town; they are not the work of an environmental agency or wildlife group. The signs are made of plywood, with letters and the profile of a turtle cut out with a jigsaw. The homemade signs—charming in their simplicity and bright colors—took someone a great deal of time and effort.

Whoever that someone was possessed the grace of spirit and generosity of heart to realize the plight of poor turtles trying to make their way across the busy road to their natural habitat.

Making and posting those simple signs was not only kind—it was prophetic.

To act "prophetically" begins with embracing what is right and just and then being willing to confront whatever seeks to destroy or obstruct that good. In baptism, God calls every one of us to the work of the prophet—to proclaim God's loving presence among his people.

In response to the priests and Levites who have come to meet him, John the Baptizer says humbly that he baptizes "with water" in anticipation of the Christ who comes. We too can give voice to the coming of the Christ in the simple "water" we have at our disposal: the water of charity, the water of comfort, the water of understanding.

It is in the simplest things we give that we most completely respond to God's prophetic call.

Meditation: When have you most recently experienced an act of kindness or generosity that you might consider a "prophetic" act?

Prayer: O Lord, with the help of your grace, may we learn to act prophetically with compassion and forgiveness. May we discern your will in the example of the prophets we encounter in our lives; may we possess the prophet's courage to "proclaim" your love in the love and compassion we give and receive.

Hugo

Readings: 1 John 2:29–3:6; John 1:29-34

Scripture:
"[T]he reason why I came baptizing with water
was that he might be made known to Israel." (John 1:31)

Reflection: Martin Scorsese's award-winning film *Hugo* is
the story of an orphan living in Paris during the 1930s. The
boy has inherited his late father's ability to fix and rebuild
things, from intricate clocks to sophisticated mechanical toys.
After his father dies, Hugo is taken in by his drunkard uncle
who is in charge of maintaining the clocks at the Paris train
station. Hugo soon masters the maze of mechanisms and
gears and keeps the clocks running with perfect precision
long after Uncle Claude disappears. Rather than be forced
to live in an orphanage, Hugo hides amid the station's lad-
ders, catwalks, and hidden passages.

A light pierces Hugo's lonely existence when he meets
Isabel, the ward of a toy shop owner. Trusting Isabel, Hugo
shows her his world of tools and gadgets, including an au-
tomaton he has inherited from his father and is trying to fix.
As he shows Isabel his secret view from the top of the great
clock tower overlooking the City of Lights, Hugo muses:

> I'd imagine the whole world was one big machine. Machines
> never come with any extra parts, you know. They always

come with the exact amount they need. So I figured, if the entire world was one big machine, I couldn't be an extra part. I had to be here for some reason . . .

Maybe that's why a broken machine always makes me a little sad, because it isn't able to do what it was meant to do . . . Maybe it's the same with people. If you lose your purpose . . . it's like you're broken.

To find our life's purpose despite our fears, our doubts, our brokenness, our feeling of inadequacy is the great challenge every one of us faces. The story of Jesus is a "schematic" for everyone in how to transform the crosses of our lives into vehicles of resurrection, to realize the purpose of our lives within the challenges and complexities we encounter, to discover wholeness and meaning as we repair and replace the broken pieces of our lives.

Meditation: As you reflect on this Christmas season, what do you see as your "purpose" in the New Year?

Prayer: Jesus, Lamb of God, help us to realize the "purpose" your Father has called us to take on in the year ahead. Mend us of our "brokenness" and restore us to hope despite our fears and doubts so that we may be about the work of reconciliation and peace you have entrusted to us.

January 4: Saint Elizabeth Ann Seton

Thrift Store Saints

Readings: 1 John 3:7-10; John 1:35-42

Scripture:
Jesus turned and saw them following him and said to them,
  "What are you looking for?"
They said to him, "Rabbi" (which translated means Teacher),
  "where are you staying?"
He said to them, "Come, and you will see." (John 1:38-39)

Reflection: Fifteen years ago, Jane Knuth, a math teacher and mom, began volunteering at the St. Vincent de Paul thrift shop in Kalamazoo, Michigan. She approached the work with typical baby-boomer hard-charging determination to "fix the world"—but over the years, the experience changed her.

Jane Knuth has collected stories of her experiences at "St. Vinnie's" in a delightful book, *Thrift Store Saints: Meeting Jesus 25¢ at a Time.* Knuth writes:

> At our meetings we frequently get into discussions about how better to run the store. . . . Eventually, it occurs to us that our purpose is not to run the most profitable, shrewd, efficient, riff-raff-free store in town. Our purpose is to help the poor and to change our own way of thinking and being. It only looks as though we run a store. The store is just our cover. . . .
> I still keep looking for "the deserving poor"—the innocent ones who are blatant victims of injustice and hard luck. I want

to help them and no one else. From what I can see, apart from children, most poor people's situations seem to stem from a mixture of uncontrollable circumstances, luck, and their own decisions. Same as my situation.

Do I deserve everything I have? Am I somehow more moral, smarter, or a harder worker than poor people? Sometimes I am, most times I'm not. Do poor people deserve their daily struggle for existence? Are they immoral, stupid, and lazy? Sometimes they are, most times they aren't.

Jane Knuth and the staff of St. Vinnie's have discovered God in the poor, the needy, the struggling who come to their store. They have embraced John's message to "Behold the Lamb of God" in their midst; they realize that the "Word made flesh" has made their dwelling in their Kalamazoo neighborhood.

The compassion of God that dawns at Christmas transforms our heart's perspective, enabling us to "see" beyond ethnic stereotypes, economic distinctions, class, and celebrity and to recognize every man, woman, and child as made in the same image and likeness of God in which we are all created.

Meditation: In what unexpected places have you discovered God making his dwelling in your midst?

Prayer: Lord Jesus, transform our vision so that we may realize your presence in every moment of this New Year. In every act of kindness, in the most hidden work for justice and reconciliation, in every extended hand and heart to those in need, may we "see" you and "hear" your call to us to discipleship and discover the work of reconciliation and justice you have set us out to do.

EPIPHANY AND
BAPTISM OF THE LORD

The Way

Readings: Isa 60:1-6; Eph 3:2-3a, 5-6; Matt 2:1-12

Scripture:
[B]ehold, magi from the east arrived in Jerusalem, saying,
"Where is the newborn king of the Jews?
We saw his star at its rising
and have come to do him homage." (Matt 2:1-2)

Reflection: Emilio Estevez's film *The Way* is the story of a father estranged from his adult son, Daniel. To his father's dismay, Daniel abandons his doctoral studies to travel the world he has only encountered in the classroom. Tom, his no-nonsense father and a successful California ophthalmologist, cannot understand why Daniel would throw his life away on wanderlust.

Daniel is killed in an accident during a freak storm in the Pyrenees while making the *Camino de Santiago de Compostela*, the centuries-old pilgrimage route to the Cathedral of St. James in Santiago, Spain. Tom goes to France to reclaim his son's body. When he learns that his son was making "the Way"—the traditional name for the pilgrimage—Tom impulsively decides to take his son's backpack and gear and complete the pilgrimage in Daniel's memory.

Though he prefers to keep to himself, Tom finds himself journeying with three other pilgrims—all very different personalities, all with their own reasons for undertaking the eight-hundred-kilometer trek: a bitter Canadian divorcee treks to St. James to quit smoking, but finds forgiveness and acceptance along the way; a gregarious Dutchman walks to shed his excess weight, but discovers the kindness and joy within him; an Irish writer is looking for a story for a novel, but rediscovers his lost faith; and Tom goes to spread Daniel's ashes, but comes to a new understanding and loving respect for his son. Their journey is not maudlin or sentimental but quietly transforming. During their trek, Tom and his fellow travelers help one another discover the difference between "the life we live and the life we choose."

Every human life is a journey in which every moment, every step is a new revelation of God's presence. In their journey to find the Christ, the magi behold the love of God in their midst (a love that the self-absorbed Herod cannot see). As Tom and his fellow travelers discover in *The Way*, our lives are journeys of discovering and encountering Emmanuel—"God with us"—in our day-to-day experiences of forgiveness, generosity, and compassion.

Meditation: In your life's journey, what has been the most difficult lesson you have learned?

Prayer: Christ Jesus, the very manifestation of God's love, be with us on our journey to your Father's dwelling place. Open our eyes to realize the "epiphanies" of your love along our "way"; illuminate the path we journey by the star of your compassion.

Demons

Readings: 1 John 3:22–4:6; Matthew 4:12-17, 23-25

Scripture:
. . . they brought to [Jesus] all who were sick with
  various diseases
and racked with pain,
those who were possessed, lunatics, and paralytics,
and he cured them. (Matt 4:24)

Reflection: The nightmares continue forty-five years after returning from Vietnam. He can't escape the memories of death and destruction. He has tried everything—drugs, alcohol, therapy—but he can't escape the memories and the images etched in his mind. *The demons of war . . .*

Her life and marriage came crashing down in betrayal and acrimony. Now she is alone and terrified at the prospect of meeting anyone and engaging in any kind of relationship. Her greatest fear is being hurt again. *The demons of brokenness . . .*

He flunked out—big time. He did not know how to handle the new responsibilities of being on his own; he couldn't manage the demands of his studies and work schedule. He's home now, working dead-end part-time jobs that he thought he had left behind forever when he graduated from high school. His mom and dad are understanding and supportive—but he knows they are disappointed and realizes the major outlay of tuition that was lost in his failed freshman year. He has no idea what to do next. *The demons of failure . . .*

Demons exist in all our lives. Traumatic experiences, emotional disasters, and shattered dreams trap us, enslave us, cripple us; these "demons" so drain us of hope that we surrender to them rather than confront them. In today's Gospel, Jesus drives out the demons that have destroyed the lives of those possessed. Jesus' healings are central to his revealing the reign of God: God's dream that no one be imprisoned or enslaved by the tragedies of life, no one be left to stumble and fall alone in the darkness. Christ calls us to the work of driving out those "demons" that divide our families, sever friendships, and rend our spirits in hopelessness and despair.

Meditation: What "demon" would you like to "drive out" of your life?

Prayer: Healing Christ, drive out of our lives the demons of division, brokenness, and fear that "possess" us and paralyze us from living our lives to the full. Help us to mend the broken, recover the lost, and heal those racked with the pain of sickness and despair. May we embrace your attitude of hope and wholeness; may we work to bring healing and joy to all in pain and distress.

January 7: Tuesday after Epiphany

Group Dynamics

Readings: 1 John 4:7-10; Mark 6:34-44

Scripture:
Then, taking the five loaves and the two fish and looking
    up to heaven,
  [Jesus] said the blessing, broke the loaves, and gave
    them to his disciples
  to set before the people;
  he also divided the two fish among them all. (Mark 6:41)

Reflection: It happens in every parish: The pastor has a new
project in mind—a religious education program for teenagers, a Thanksgiving dinner for the poor, a food drive or clothing collection for the local shelter. The pastor then approaches
parishioners to help out. It's a tough sell: people are very
protective of their time; they're not sure this is something
they want to do or are comfortable getting involved with;
they doubt they have the abilities and patience necessary for
this kind of work. But, eventually, a group of volunteers—
however reluctantly—comes together.

And then, without fail, the remarkable happens. Once the
group sees the importance of what they are doing and the
potential good they can do, they are transformed by that
realization. Their reluctance gives way to fresh optimism
and enthusiasm; their doubts disappear in a new spirit of

"anything is possible." Holding back at the beginning, they are ready to devote whatever time and skills and resources necessary to see the project through. The volunteers are caught up in the joy of doing good.

They have become a community.

They are *church.*

What happens in today's gospel is such an experience of church. Jesus transforms a gathering of many different people who become one in their need, one in the bread they share, one in the love of Jesus who has brought them together. Taking the few pieces of bread and fish they can collect, Christ works a miracle. Christ empowers each one of us to perform our own miracles of creating community when we give of our time and resources to take on the work of the gospel: feeding the hungry, caring for the sick, seeking out the lost and forgotten, teaching to all the good news that God is our loving Father. In doing so, we create the "miracle" of becoming *church.*

Meditation: In addition to the Eucharist, in what ways do you experience being part of "church"?

Prayer: As you give to us, O God, may we give to one another. May our humble acts of generosity and forgiveness become visible signs of your invisible grace. Let our everyday efforts at reconciliation and healing transform our simplest offerings into sacraments of your love, and so become your church for our broken, expectant world.

January 8: Wednesday after Epiphany

Grace in the Midst of a Storm

Readings: 1 John 4:11-18; Mark 6:45-52

Scripture:
"Take courage, it is I, do not be afraid!" (Mark 6:50)

Reflection: Liam Doyle came into the world with an incomplete heart: he was born without one of the four chambers needed for the muscle to pump blood through his little body. Twice before the age of two, Liam underwent open-heart surgery to rebuild his heart. It was a terrifying ordeal for Mary and Brian, his mom and dad. But Brian Doyle writes in his book *Leaping: Revelations and Epiphanies* that the family's traumatic experience was also a rare occasion of grace:

> The first operation was terrifying, but it happened so fast and was so necessary and was so soon after the day [Liam] was born with a twin brother that we all—mother, father, sister, families, friends—staggered through the days and nights too tired and frightened to do anything but lurch into the next hour.
>
> But by the second operation my son was nearly two years old, a stubborn, funny, amiable boy with a crooked gunslinger's grin, and when a doctor carried him down the hall, his moon-boy face grinning at me as it receded toward awful pain and possible death, I went somewhere dark that frightens me still. It was a cold black country that I hope to never see again. Yet out of the dark came my wife's hand like a

hawk, and I believe, to this hour, that when she touched me I received pure grace. She woke me, saved me, not for the first time, not for the last.

In all the storms we experience in our lives, Christ makes his calming presence known: Someone's generosity helps us steady our sinking craft; the wisdom of another who has sailed this same difficult route shows us the way through; family and friends stay up with us through the terrifying watches of the night. In these good souls, the light of Christ illuminates the night; his peace, experienced in their support, steadies our craft. In them, Christ rescues us.

Christ asks us to be his presence to others struggling to stay afloat in their own rough seas. In our own generous outreach, may others hear the assurance of Jesus: "Take courage, it is I, do not be afraid!"

Meditation: What was the last "storm" you encountered, and how did Christ appear to help you make your way to safety?

Prayer: Come, Lord, and board our small boats. Quiet the winds that batter our lives; calm the seas that threaten to sink us. May your forgiveness and peace balance our crafts for the journey to your harbor and enable us to help others survive the gales and tumultuous seas encountered in every life's voyage.

January 9: Thursday after Epiphany

"We 'Do' Cancer . . ."

Readings: 1 John 4:19–5:4; Luke 4:14-22

Scripture:
> *The Spirit of the Lord is upon me,*
> *because he has anointed me*
> *to bring glad tidings to the poor . . .* (Luke 4:18)

Reflection: In her best-selling memoir *My Grandfather's Blessings*, Rachel Naomi Remen relates the story of Celia and Richard. Richard was a widower; his wife had suffered a long and painful death from cancer. Then he met Celia; they came to love each other and each other's children dearly. But less than a year into their courtship, Celia discovered a lump in her breast. Without telling Richard, she underwent tests and learned the devastating news from her doctor: the lump was malignant.

Not wanting to put Richard and his children through such an ordeal again, Celia broke off their relationship. She gave no reason or explanation. After refusing his phone calls for weeks, Celia finally relented and agreed to meet Richard. When they met, she could see the deep strain and hurt on his face. Richard gently asked Celia why she had broken up with him. Finally, on the verge of tears, she told Richard about her diagnosis, about her surgery, about the protocol of chemotherapy she was about to begin.

"You and the children have lived through this once already," she told him, "I won't put you through it again."

He looked at her, openmouthed. "You have cancer?" he asked. She nodded, the tears beginning to run down her cheeks.

"Oh, Celia," he said—and began to laugh with relief. "We can do cancer . . . we know how to do cancer. I thought that you didn't love me."*

Oh, but she did. And they got through it together, happily married.

The Gospel of compassion and reconciliation is "fulfilled" every time we imitate the selfless giving of Jesus. Whether we can "do cancer," whether we know how to comfort and console another, whether we can make a soup kitchen or a tutoring program work, we make Isaiah's vision a reality in our own Nazareths. As disciples of Jesus, we inherit the Spirit's call to "bring glad tidings" and "proclaim the Lord's favor" to the poor, the imprisoned, the blind, the oppressed, and the helpless.

Meditation: What do you "do" well—no matter how small or insignificant it seems—that can reveal of the Spirit of God in your "hearing"?

Prayer: May your Spirit come upon us, O God, that we may help others see your presence in all our lives, that we may bring hope and healing to broken relationships and old hurts, that we may be freed from the distractions and detours that impede our search for you.

Lepers

Readings: 1 John 5:5-13; Luke 5:12-16

Scripture:
   [The leper] fell prostrate, pleaded with [Jesus], and said,
   "Lord, if you wish, you can make me clean."
Jesus stretched out his hand, touched him, and said,
   "I do will it. Be made clean." (Luke 5:12-13)

Reflection: In modern medicine, leprosy is called Hansen's disease, a bacterial disease that attacks the nerves of the hands and feet, the eyes, and the face. It is rare and not very contagious—and since 1981 curable.

   But in Jesus' time, any skin rash, discoloration, or disfigurement was considered leprosy. Lepers then were considered contagious; contact with a leper required extensive bathing and laundering; anything that came into contact with a leper was destroyed. Those considered lepers were sent away from the city or town. Many believed that leprosy was a punishment from God for sin. The real disease of leprosy, it seems, was the fear lepers engendered in others.

   Jesus' curing of lepers shocked those who witnessed the healings. Jesus did not drive the leper away, as would be the norm (the leper, according to the Mosaic Law, had no right to even address Jesus); instead, Jesus stretched out his hand and touched him. Jesus did not see an unclean leper but a human soul in desperate need.

We let fear, anger, and distrust create "lepers" in our own time and place. We exile these lepers to the margins of society outside our gates; we diminish these lepers to simple stereotypes and demeaning labels; we reject these lepers as too "unclean" to be part of our lives and our world. We are terrified of becoming identified ourselves with their "leprosy."

The Christ who healed lepers comes to perform a much greater miracle—to heal us of our debilitating sense of self that fails to realize the sacred dignity of those we demean as or reduce to "lepers." Jesus calls us who would be his disciples to let our own "miracles" of charity and mercy, of forgiveness and justice, be "proof" of our committed discipleship to the gospel and our trust in the God who is the real worker of wonders in our midst.

Meditation: Who are the "lepers" in your town and village? What makes them "lepers" that causes people to shun and reject them? How can you view them as "clean"?

Prayer: Father of compassion, heal us of our blindness that disables us from seeing one another as your children; remove the hardness from our hearts that prevents us from embracing one another as brothers and sisters. May we speak Jesus' word and extend his hand to one another in order to clean and be cleaned of the leprosy of arrogance, pride, and hatred.

The Best Man

Readings: 1 John 5:14-21; John 3:22-30

Scripture:
[John said:]
"The one who has the bride is the bridegroom;
the best man, who stands and listens for him,
rejoices greatly at the bridegroom's voice.
So this joy of mine has been made complete.
He must increase; I must decrease." (John 3:29-30)

Reflection: Today is the last day of the church's liturgical celebration of Christmas. The gospel reading for today is, fittingly, the final appearance of John the Baptizer in the Fourth Gospel.

The portrait of John in the Fourth Gospel is quite different from the fiery preacher and eccentric we meet in the gospels of Mark, Matthew, and Luke. The John of the Fourth Gospel is not the Baptizer of the wild visage, camel skins, and locusts and wild honey. The John we read about today is self-effacing and subdued. He diverts any attention away from himself to focus entirely on his testimony to the "light." John is completely dedicated to showing others the way to Jesus the "Lamb of God"; his joy is in helping others discover the presence of God in their midst.

In today's gospel, Jesus has begun his teaching ministry. John realizes that his work is done; he graciously takes his leave with gratitude to God for entrusting him to be "best man" for his Son and for "completing" his joy in the dawning of God's Christ.

"He must increase; I must decrease." John's final words in the Fourth Gospel might well be our prayer as we begin this New Year. The Baptizer in the Fourth Gospel models the humble, selfless spirit of servanthood that Jesus will proclaim in his teachings, in his signs and miracles, and, ultimately, in his passion, death, and resurrection. To walk with Jesus in the coming year means embracing John's attitude of selflessness: to place ourselves last for the sake of others; to seek reconciliation and peace before the satisfaction of our own needs and egos; to work to establish God's kingdom of compassion and justice before securing our own needs and security. In doing so, rather than finding ourselves wanting, we will find our "complete" joy.

Meditation: What, in your life, might "decrease" so that the love of God might "increase" in the year ahead?

Prayer: O God, as we conclude our celebration of your Son's birth, help us to embrace the spirit of humility and generosity of your herald John so that we might become prophets of your Son's presence in our midst. May our needs and wants, our fears and doubts, "decrease" so that your compassion, justice, and forgiveness may "increase" in this New Year.

Chosen

Readings: Isa 42:1-4, 6-7; Acts 10:34-38; Matt 3:13-17

Scripture:
After Jesus was baptized,
　　he came up from the water and behold,
　　the heavens were opened for him,
　　and he saw the Spirit of God descending like a dove
　　and coming upon him.
And a voice came from the heavens, saying,
　　"This is my beloved Son, with whom I am well
　　　pleased." (Matt 3:16-17)

Reflection: Your son or daughter comes to you. "Dad, I'm not getting this math problem." "Mom, I think this boy likes me." Whether you realize it or not, *you have been chosen.*

The parish office calls. "Your friends Sheila and Peg were raving about the beautiful floral displays you made for the garden club. We were wondering if you might help us with decorating the church this Easter." *You*—with your green thumb and creative flair—*have been chosen.*

The recent storm did a great deal of damage to houses in your neighborhood. The small yard of the older couple next door is covered with tree limbs and debris. You have a couple of free hours this afternoon. So get the wheelbarrow out and the chain saw gassed up—*you have been chosen.*

Things are unfair. The situation is untenable. Changes have to be made—a plan needs to be developed, resources identified. But, first, someone has to come forward to lead the effort. The anger that motivates you, the empathy you feel for the hurting and victimized, your experience that has taught you what needs to happen to make things right—listen to that voice pushing you. *You have been chosen.*

At his baptism, Jesus fully realizes that he is loved and chosen by God for a mission that only he can fulfill. In our own baptisms, we realize that God has chosen us and we accept his call to be about his work of reconciliation. God chooses us, his beloved, now, in the lives we live; he has given us everything we need to respond: a spirit of compassion and justice, an empathetic heart, a commitment to bring God's reconciling love into our lives and the lives of those we love.

Meditation: What work or task in the New Year do you sense God has "chosen" you to complete—and why *you*?

Prayer: O God, in the waters of baptism you have raised us up and set us on our life's journey to your dwelling place. May your Spirit come upon us to inspire us and guide us in the work of reconciliation and justice you have chosen us to undertake. May the spring of your life within us make currents of your compassion and peace for all.

References

Introduction
Phillips Brooks, "O Little Town of Bethlehem" (1867).

December 5: Thursday of the First Week of Advent
Pat Brady and Don Wimmer, *Rose Is Rose* (Kansas City, MO: 1999). Copyright 1999 by Pat Brady and Don Wimmer. Reprinted by permission of Universal Uclick for UFS. All rights reserved.

December 6: Friday of the First Week of Advent
Nora Gallagher, *The Sacred Meal* (Nashville, TN: Thomas Nelson, 2009), 39–40.

December 8: Second Sunday of Advent
Kathleen Norris, *Acedia & Me: A Marriage, Monks, and a Writer's Life* (New York: Riverhead Books, 2008), 223.

December 9: The Immaculate Conception of the Blessed Virgin Mary
Lauren F. Winner, Living by the Word, "Interrupted," *The Christian Century* (December 16, 2008): 20.

December 16: Monday of the Third Week of Advent
Gabrielle Giffords and Mark Kelly, with Jeffrey Zaslow, *Gabby: A Story of Courage and Hope* (New York: Scribner, 2011), 89.

December 23: Monday in Late Advent
Denise Roy, *My Monastery Is a Minivan: Where the Daily Is Divine and the Routine Becomes Prayer* (Chicago: Loyola Press, 2001), 45–46.